SUPER
SURPRISING
TRiViA
ABOUT
the
PARANORMAL

by Megan Cooley Peterson

CAPSTONE PRESS
a capstone imprint

Spark is published by Capstone Press, an imprint of Capstone
1710 Roe Crest Drive, North Mankato, Minnesota 56003
capstonepub.com

Library of Congress Cataloging-in-Publication Data is available on the
Library of Congress website.
ISBN: 9781669064855 (hardcover)
ISBN: 9781669071754 (paperback)
ISBN: 9781669064879 (ebook PDF)

Summary: Think you know all there is to know about paranormal
mysteries? Prepare to learn even more! From ghost ships to UFOs to
haunted dolls, discover tantalizing trivia about mysteries that have haunted
humanity for hundreds of years in this totally spooky book of paranormal
trivia.

Editorial Credits
Editor: Mandy Robbins; Designer: Heidi Thompson; Media Researcher:
Jo Miller; Production Specialist: Tori Abraham

Image Credits
Alamy: Chronicle, 20, 25, William Silver, 12; Getty Images: Barry King,
18, bauhaus1000, 11, Bettmann, 9 (bottom), 26, Express, 15, Topical
Press Agency, 14; Library of Congress, 8, 9 (top), 10; Shutterstock: Anna
Kucherova, 5, Art fantasy, 16, David Buzzard, 13, Dmitrijs Bindemanis,
17, Everett Collection, 6, 7, ex_artist, 24; HUT Design, Cover (right),
Joeprachatree, 22, ktsdesign, Cover (top left), Noel V. Baebler, 4, photoBeard,
19, Raggedstone, Cover (bottom left), Squeeb Creative, Cover (middle left),
Ursatii, 29, WindVector, 27; TopFoto: Fortean, 23, World History Archive, 21;
U.S. Air Force photo by Senior Airman Roslyn Ward, 28

TABLE OF CONTENTS

Words in **bold** are in the glossary.

DO YOU BELIEVE?

Do **ghosts** hang around the White House? Are aliens real? Can dolls be **haunted**? The **paranormal** world can't easily be explained. What you discover in this book might make you a believer!

WHITE HOUS GHOSTS

Do ghosts nap at the White House? Visitors say Andrew Jackson's spirit does. The former president snoozes in the Queen's Bedroom.

First Lady Abigail Adams hung laundry in the East Room. She died in 1818. Staff sometimes smell clean laundry there.

Abraham Lincoln's ghost often appeared in the Lincoln Bedroom at the White House. British Prime Minister Winston Churchill saw the ghostly president by the fireplace. Maybe the ghost was cold.

The Netherland's Queen Wilhelmina stayed there too. She saw Lincoln's ghost. He knocked on the door wearing his top hat.

President Ronald Reagan's dog wouldn't enter the Lincoln Bedroom. It barked at the door.

A strange ghost made a brief White House appearance when William H. Taft was president. This happened in 1911. Staff members called it "The Thing." It often touched their shoulders.

David Burns once owned the land the White House is on. His ghost might haunt the Yellow Oval Room. A worker once heard a voice say, "I am Burns."

HAUNTED DOLLS

Robert the Doll lives in a museum in Florida. People say Robert is haunted. He moves on his own. Cameras stop working when people try to take Robert's photo.

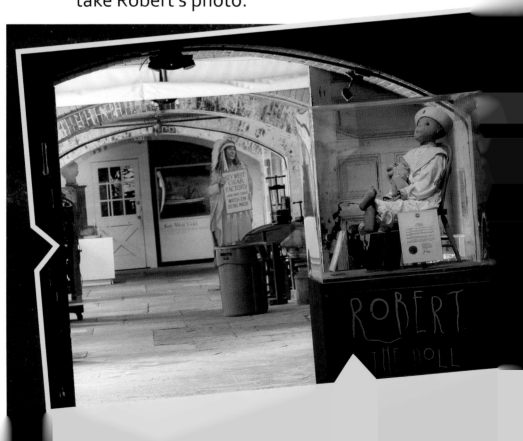

A doll named Mandy scares visitors at the Quesnel Museum in Canada. Her eyes blink.

SEAWORTHY SPIRITS

The *Titanic* sank in 1912. Captain Edward Smith's body was never found. His ghost has appeared at his former home in England.

The *Queen Mary* is a floating hotel. More than 40 people have died onboard. Guests say ghosts turn on faucets. They rip off bedsheets.

The *Lady Lovibond* sank in the English Channel in 1748. Every 50 years, the ghost ship is said to sail again. People have reported a green glow around the ghostly ship.

Legends say dead sailors crew the *Flying Dutchman* ghost ship. No one knows if this ship ever existed. *Dutchman* stories have been told since at least the 1600s.

ALIENS FROM OUTER SPACE

Area 51 is an **Air Force base** in Nevada.

Does the U.S. government hide aliens there?

Some people think so.

A man named Robert Lazar said he saw photos of aliens kept at Area 51.

Barney and Betty Hill said aliens took them in 1961. The Hills said the aliens had gray skin and huge eyes. While they were gone, their watches stopped.

Betty later found pink powder on her dress. The powder stumped scientists. Did aliens leave it?

In 1977, a craft landed near a school in Wales in the United Kingdom. Some children saw an alien. It wore a silver suit.

Students in Zimbabwe shared their playground with aliens in 1994. The kids said two aliens climbed out of a silver ship. They had big eyes.

FLYING SAUCERS

John Martin reported a saucer-like **UFO** near Denison, Texas, in 1878. He was one of the first people to call UFOs "saucers."

In 1951, a UFO with blue lights flew all over Texas. The lights formed a V-shape. Many people saw them.

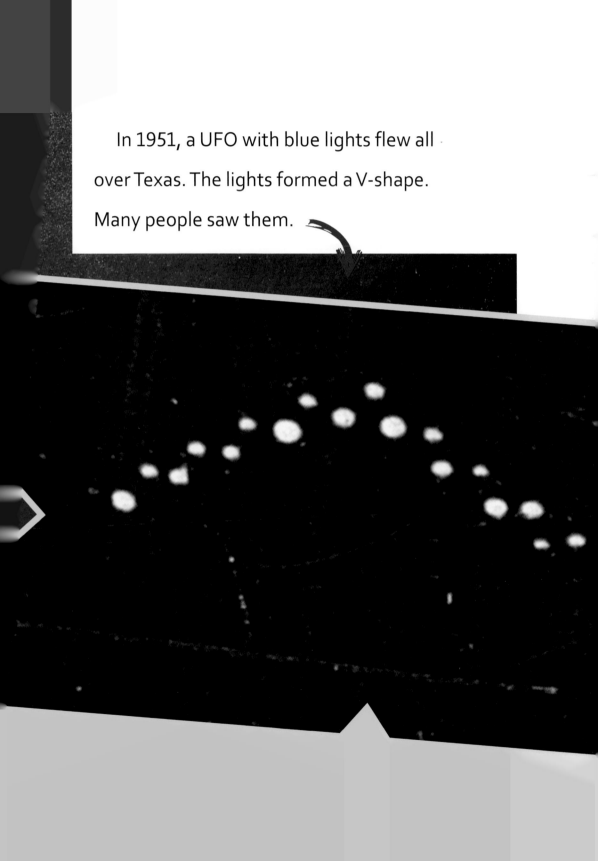

A farmer found crashed UFO pieces near Roswell, New Mexico, in 1947. He found rubber strips, tinfoil, and heavy paper.

The U.S. Army said the pieces were from a weather balloon. Some people believe the Roswell UFO is kept at Area 51.

Many **Navy** pilots think they share the sky with UFOs. The crafts have no wings. They fly faster than any plane.

In 2021, the U.S. government studied 144 past UFO sightings. One turned out to be a weather balloon. The other 143 remain unsolved.

Glossary

Air Force (AYR FORS)—the part of the U.S. military that's trained to fight with aircraft

base (BAYS)—an area run by the military where people serving in the military live and military supplies are stored

ghost (GOHST)—a spirit of a dead person believed to haunt people or places

haunt (HAWNT)—to cause unexplained events to occur or appear as a ghost in a certain place

legend (LEJ-uhnd)—a story passed down through the years that may not be completely true

Navy (NAY-vee)—the military sea force of a country

paranormal (pair-uh-NOR-muhl)—having to do with an unexplained event that has no scientific explanation

UFO (YOO-EF-OH)—an object in the sky thought to be a spaceship from another planet; UFO is short for Unidentified Flying Object

Read More

Bolte, Mari. *Area 51 and Other Top Secret Science*. Ann Arbor, MI: Cherry Lake Publishing Group, 2023.

Katz, Susan B. *Famous Ghosts*. Minneapolis: Lerner Publications, 2024.

Peterson, Megan Cooley. *Spotting UFOs with Tech*. North Mankato, MN: Capstone Press, 2024.

Internet Sites

Alien Investigation Primary Source
natgeokids.com/uk/primary-resource/alien-investigation-primary-resource/

Ghost Research Society
ghostresearch.org/

NASA. Kids' Club
nasa.gov/kidsclub/index.html

Index

About the Author

Megan Cooley Peterson is a children's book author and editor. When not writing, Megan enjoys movies, books, and all things Halloween. She lives in Minnesota with her husband and daughter.